I0760094

DOGS vs. HUMANS

A Showdown of the Senses

To Kyra and Connor, for starting it all in the first place — S.G.
For Sienna, who loves all dogs, even (especially!) the weird ones — B.E.

A mastiff-sized thank you to Stacey Roderick and the entire Owlkids team for collaborating with me on this book. Tail wags to Bambi Edlund for the accurate and adorable illustrations. And endless woofs of appreciation to my agent, Jacqui Lipton; my critique partners; and my entire family for all their support – S.G.

Owlkids Books acknowledges the financial support of the Canada Council for the Arts, the Ontario Arts Council, the Government of Canada through the Canada Book Fund (CBF) and the Government of Ontario through the Ontario Creates Book Initiative for our publishing activities.

Owlkids Books gratefully acknowledges that our office in Toronto is located on the traditional territory of many nations, including the Mississaugas of the Credit, the Chippewa, the Wendat, the Anishinaabeg, and the Haudenosaunee Peoples.

Published in Canada by Owlkids Books Inc., 1 Eglinton Avenue East, Toronto, ON M4P 3A1
Published in the US by Owlkids Books Inc., 819 Bancroft Way, Berkeley, CA 94710

Library of Congress Control Number: 2024938854

Library and Archives Canada Cataloguing in Publication
Title: Dogs vs. humans : a showdown of the senses / written by Stephanie Gibeault ; illustrated by Bambi Edlund.
Other titles: Dogs versus humans
Names: Gibeault, Stephanie, author. | Edlund, Bambi, illustrator.
Identifiers: Canadiana (print) 20240377796 | Canadiana (ebook) 2024037780X | ISBN 9781771475785 (hardcover) | ISBN 9781771477215 (EPUB)
Subjects: LCSH: Senses and sensation—Juvenile literature. | LCSH: Dogs—Sense organs—Juvenile literature. | LCSH: Physiology, Comparative—Juvenile literature. | LCGFT: Instructional and educational works. | LCGFT: Illustrated works.
Classification: LCC QP434 .G55 2025 | DDC j573.6/7—dc23

Edited by Stacey Roderick | Designed by Danielle Arbour

Manufactured in Guangdong, Dongguan, China, in August 2024, by Toppan Leefung Packaging & Printing (Dongguan) Co., Ltd
Job #BAYDC138

hc A B C D E F

Owlkids Books is a division of

DOGS vs. HUMANS

A Showdown of the Senses

Written by Stephanie Gibeault **Illustrated by Bambi Edlund**

Owlkids Books

DOGS can do some incredible things, like find hikers lost deep in the woods or spot intruders sneaking around in the dark.

How do they do it? They use their keen senses!

Long ago, before they became the pets we know today, dogs were wolves. And their senses had developed in ways that helped them survive in the wild. For example, they used their senses to protect themselves from danger, search for food and water, and find their way home. That past still shapes the way dogs experience the world today. Only now, they mostly use their senses for more fun activities, like spotting squirrels *waaay* across the park and hunting down unattended hamburgers.

When a dog's senses detect something such as that delicious hamburger, they send messages to her brain. Then her brain tells her body what to do in response to the information: "That burger on the picnic table looks and smells like it's going to taste really good. Go for it!"

FIDO FACT: Dogs evolved from wolves at least 15,000 years ago.

Each person and dog senses the world in their own unique way. You might have a terrific sense of smell while somebody else has anosmia, meaning they are unable to smell. One dog can be born without sight while another works as a guide dog for blind or partially sighted people. In this book, we are talking about how the senses of dogs and people work *in general*.

We humans experience our environment through our senses too. They allow us to enjoy our favorite TV shows and know what's cooking for dinner before we're told — and *also* to avoid danger and find our way home.

So since both dogs and humans see, smell, taste, feel, and hear their way around the world, who do you think would win in a showdown of the senses? Who would spot that squirrel first? And who would smell every ingredient in dinner? Let's find out if dogs will be crowned top dog or if humans will win the prize.

Who SEES It Better?

Lots of humans wear glasses, but not very many dogs do! That must mean dogs are the clear winners when it comes to vision, right? Well, let's just see about that ...

You might be surprised to learn that when it comes to seeing details in the distance, humans run circles around dogs. In fact, if a person with average vision can see something clearly from the length of a city bus away, a dog would need to stand much closer — just the length of a small car — to be able to see it as well.

So how do dogs spot those squirrels scurrying around at the other end of the park? Dogs' eyes are built for detecting movement! From far away, dogs can recognize objects that are moving better than objects that are still. This ability helped their wolf ancestors spot and chase running prey.

Our eyes face forward, but most dog breeds have eyes that face slightly out to the sides. This difference gives humans more overlap between what their two eyes can see. That means better depth perception, which is what allows you to reach out and pick up a glass of water without knocking it over or missing it entirely.

Here's an eye-opening fact: dogs can see in the dark because they have a special mirror-like layer at the back of their eyes! That's why their eyes seem to glow in the dark when you shine a light at them — it's actually the light being bounced back. This layer reflects the light, which gives their eyes a second chance to absorb it. So dogs can see with much less light than humans need.

Dogs can see colors, just not all the colors of the rainbow that a human can. To a dog, the world is made up of shades of yellow, blue, and gray. That means what looks like a red ball on green grass to a person, looks like a yellow ball on yellow grass to a dog.

FIDO FACT: Puppies don't open their eyes and see until they're about two weeks old.

Dog	VISION	Human
0	Distance vision	1
0	Depth perception	1
0	Color vision	1
1	Night vision	0

Who SMELLS It Better?

Dogs are famous for their powerful and lifesaving noses. Some can even sniff out people buried in an avalanche or smell an illness before a doctor has diagnosed it! Seems like the winner of this contest might be right under your nose ...

The fact is, a dog's nose is thousands and *thousands* of times more sensitive than any human's! Why? Dogs have millions more smell-sensing cells in their noses. They use a larger part of their brains for identifying odors too. And when they take a breath, some of the air is used *only* for smelling, while humans send all their air to their lungs for breathing.

This means a dog could sniff out a *single* strip of bacon in a sports stadium filled with oranges! A human likely couldn't manage that even if the bacon was only in a bathtub full of oranges.

A dog's round nostrils have narrow slits at the corners. When he breathes out, these slits send the exhaled air to the sides rather than straight ahead. That means odors in front of the dog's nose can be inhaled with his next breath instead of being blown away. The slits also cause the exhaled air to swirl around, kicking up nearby odors that might be on the ground. Then the dog can sniff those stirred-up scent particles on his next breath in.

FIDO FACT: Dogs' noseprints are like human fingerprints. Each one is unique.

It's no surprise that dogs use their powerful noses to find treats, but did you know they also use them to communicate? That's right! Dogs use smells to send and receive messages.

Every dog's rear end has a unique smell, which is why dogs say hello by sniffing each other's butts. It's kind of like finding out another dog's name. (Thank goodness humans use their words!)

Sniffing each other's pee also tells dogs a lot, such as another dog's age, whether that dog is male or female, and whether that dog is healthy or sick. That's why our furry friends make sure to check the pee-mail at the local fire hydrant!

Dog	SMELL	Human
1	Detecting smells	0
1	Communicating by smell	0

Who TASTES It Better?

Some people eat strong-tasting foods, such as stinky cheeses or hot peppers. But then again, some dogs eat poop and dirty socks. Surely humans will taste victory in this contest ...

Both dogs and people sense taste through teeny organs called taste buds. They are found mostly on the tongue and send signals to the brain about how something tastes. Humans have five thousand to eight thousand taste buds. Compare that to a dog's measly one thousand seven hundred. No wonder dogs eat things you wouldn't even consider tasting!

Scientists think dogs have a good reason for some of their not-so-picky eating habits. Early dogs were most likely scavengers. That means they partly survived by eating waste left behind by humans. So a dog's taste for poop and garbage is just part of her nature.

Both dogs and humans can taste whether a food is sweet, salty, sour, bitter, or savory. But just as you might prefer sugary candy to mouth-puckering lemonade, dogs have favorite tastes too.

All dogs think meat is fan-*taste*-tic, thanks to the hunting habits of their predatory wolf relatives. And they have lots of taste buds that sense sweetness, so many dogs also love a variety of vegetables and fruit. But it's pretty certain you won't find a dog who enjoys bitter or sour foods. That's the taste of many spoiled or poisonous foods, so dogs' ancestors learned long ago to avoid them for safety.

A dog would never ask you to pass the salt either. Their tongues aren't very sensitive to the taste of salt. Even though dogs, like humans, need a certain amount of salt to be healthy, they generally don't

seek it out in their diet. Remember that they evolved to eat meat, which is a naturally salty food.

Dogs *can* taste something you can't, though — pure water! It's believed that humans can't actually taste water, just the minerals that are in it. But scientists think dogs have taste buds on the tips of their tongues that are specifically for tasting water. Slurp!

Dog	TASTE	Human
0	Number of taste buds	1
0	Salt tasting	1
1	Water tasting	0

ROUND 4 Who FEELS It Better?

Let's get in touch with another sense: *touch*. Both dogs and humans feel things with their skin, but except for a few hairless breeds, dogs are covered in thick fur. So *fur* sure, they can't feel more than humans can. Or can they ... ?

Q: What did the whisker say to the dog?

A: Let's keep in touch.

When dogs feel pain, they often try to hide it so they don't look weak. This is another behavior that comes from their wolf ancestors. In the wild, sick or hurt animals are often picked on or attacked.

Furry or not, skin is loaded with touch receptors. These receptors are special nerve endings that detect sensations such as pressure, texture, and temperature. Then they send that information to the brain.

But the bare skin on dogs' noses does some extra-special sensing. A dog's nose can feel the faint body heat of people or animals from as much as 5 ft. (1.5 m) away! That's about the length of a park bench. This ability probably helped dogs' wolf ancestors find the warm bodies of hidden prey when they were hunting.

When it comes to touch, dogs might just win the competition by a hair — their whiskers! These stiff, thick hairs that grow around a dog's muzzle, jaws, and eyes help him sense the shape and size of objects near his face. Whiskers are sort of like an early-warning system to stop a dog from banging into things, which is especially useful in the dark.

How do whiskers work? When one bends from touching something, it causes a touch sensor deep under the skin to send a message to the dog's brain. Even the air moving around an object can bend these wiry hairs enough to alert the dog that there's something close by.

FIDO FACT: A dog's paws have oodles of touch receptors. That's why many dogs don't like their sensitive paws being touched.

Dog	TOUCH	Human
1	Heat-sensitive noses	0
1	Extrasensory whiskers	0

Who HEARS It Better?

Compared with humans, dogs have pretty big ears. All the better to hear with, right? But better than humans? We need to give this a fair *hearing* ...

Humans can actually make out low-pitched sounds, such as the deep thumping of bass drums, a bit better than dogs. But when it comes to high-pitched sounds, such as whistles, dogs are super *hear*-oes! In fact, many sounds that are too high for people to hear, such as the squeak of a rodent or the chirp of an insect, are loud and clear to dogs. Scientists think that the ability to hear high-pitched sounds might have helped dogs' wolf ancestors find small prey in the brush.

Q: Why was the basset hound such a good piano player?
A: She learned to play by ear.

When people hear an unexpected noise, they usually turn toward the sound. Dogs do the same thing, but they don't have to move their whole head to pinpoint where the noise is coming from. They can move just their ears toward the sound — and they can even move each one in a different direction, if needed!

You might think all that ear action would give dogs the upper paw. But it turns out that humans are better at finding the exact location of a sound. This might be because locating a sound with the ears helps the eyes find its source. And since we humans have better distance vision than dogs, we might also have developed the ability to zero in on sounds more accurately.

FIDO FACT: Puppies don't hear well until they're about three weeks old.

Dog	HEARING	Human
0	Hearing low-pitched sounds	1
1	Hearing high-pitched sounds	0
0	Locating sounds	1

BONUS Round

Before we end this showdown, let's explore a lesser-known sense —magnetoreception. This is the ability to detect the Earth's magnetic field. How is this helpful? Dogs can use this sense to find their way home, even if they're in an unfamiliar neighborhood. A dog uses his magnetoreception to identify the north and south poles, which, along with information from his other senses, helps him decide which direction to travel in.

And guess what? A recent scientific study suggests that humans likely have the same sense. But this information is so new that nobody knows for sure yet how—or if—people use magnetoreception.

Dogs' wolf ancestors would have used magnetoreception to find their way around huge territories. Today's dogs are still so in tune with the Earth's magnetic poles that they often line themselves up in a north–south direction when they poop!

Do dogs have any senses people don't? They seem to when they react in ways we don't understand. For example, some dogs know when a human is feeling sick and will stay by that person's side. How can they know what that human is feeling? Body odor! When you're sick, the chemicals in your body change, and that transforms the way you smell. You might not notice the subtle difference, but dogs sure can.

How about predicting disasters? There are stories of dogs becoming restless hours or even days before an earthquake strikes. It's tempting to imagine they are predicting the tremors with an extra sense. But some scientists think it's more likely their senses are simply detecting things human senses can't, such as the smell of gases released from deep in the Earth or the high-pitched sound of rocks grinding together.

So no, dogs don't have extra senses — or at least not ones scientists have discovered yet.

Q: Did you hear about the dog who could predict earthquakes?

A: Yes, it was ground-breaking news.

And the Winner of the Showdown of the Senses Is ...

Even though dogs can see better in the dark, the human eyes have it — people win the vision round. Of course, dogs are *far* superior smellers, which is nothing to sniff at. A human's taste buds take the cake — except when it comes to water. A dog's sense of touch feels trophy-worthy. And apart from high-pitched sounds, humans are best in class at hearing.

But here's the real final score: dogs are great at being dogs, and humans are great at being humans. Although dogs and people share the same environment, we adapted differently and so we sense the world differently. The next time you see a dog, think about what you have learned about her senses. Then any surprising doggy behavior — from eating dirty socks to barking for no apparent reason — will make perfect sense.

Words to Know

Ancestor: A family member from a very long time ago.

Anosmia: The partial or complete loss of the sense of smell.

Depth perception: The ability to see the world in three dimensions (depth, length, and width) and judge the distance between objects.

Dog breed: Groups of dogs that have been developed by people to share similar characteristics. Beagles and Labrador retrievers are examples of dog breeds.

Magnetoreception: The ability to sense the Earth's magnetic poles without using a tool such as a compass.

Muzzle: An animal's snout including the nose and mouth.

Perception: An awareness of something using a sense or senses.

Predator: An animal that hunts other animals for food.

Prey: An animal that is hunted by other animals for food.

Receptor: A special cell or group of cells that sense stimuli like light or heat.

Savory: The "meaty" flavor found in foods such as meat, miso, or mushrooms.

Scavenger: An animal whose diet includes dead animals, rotting plants, or garbage.

Taste buds: The tiny organs on the tongue and in the mouth that provide the sense of taste.